MUSIC THROUGH TIME

PAUL HARRIS & SALLY ADAMS

FLUTE BOOK 1

Christopher Columbus returned from his final voyage. Fifteenth-century geography was still a bit haphazard, and he died the following year in obscurity, believing the New World he had discovered—America—was off the coast of China!

Josquin was the greatest composer of the Renaissance, famous enough in his day to have his portrait painted by Leonardo da Vinci. 'El Grillo' is Spanish for 'the cricket', and this piece was originally a partsong about the insect's love of singing.

1505
El Grillo

Josquin Desprès
(c.1440–1521)

Bartholomew Legate and Edward Wightman were the last people to be burned at the stake for heresy in England. Also in England, a flag was flown at half-mast for the first time to signify a death—though not, sadly, that of the two unfortunate heretics.

This piece is from a set of dances Praetorius compiled for the Duke of Brunswick. He named the collection *Terpsichore*, after the Greek Muse of dancing.

1612
Gavotte

Michael Praetorius
(1571–1612)

Printed in Great Britain
OXFORD UNIVERSITY PRESS, MUSIC DEPARTMENT, GREAT CLARENDON STREET, OXFORD OX2 6DP

1714
March

George Frideric Handel
(1685–1759)

Queen Anne died, having been the first monarch to rule over Great Britain after the Union of England and Scotland. She had had 17 children, all of whom died before they grew up, and was so fat when she was crowned that she had to be carried to her throne.

Though born in Germany, Handel lived for much of his life in England. With the composer Bononcini he founded the original Royal Academy of Music, a risky business venture to stage opera.

1720
Bella Vittoria

Antonio Maria Bononcini
(1677–1726)

Wallpaper became fashionable in Britain. There was an early Stock Market crash when the 'South Sea Bubble'—a wild craze of financial speculation in the South Seas Trading Company—finally burst.

The composer of this piece was the brother of Handel's one-time business partner (see the previous piece): music was the Bononcini family business, with father and all three sons well-known composers.

Dr Samuel Johnson's *Dictionary of the English Language* appeared, the culmination of eight years' work. Unlike today's dictionaries, it contained only what he considered the 'best' words, defined with the aid of his prodigious memory and witty personal views.

Oswald was a Scottish composer, dancing master, string player, and publisher. This piece is taken from his collection of *Airs for the Four Seasons*.

1755
Minuet

James Oswald
(c.1711–1769)

Mozart died this year, in circumstances that are still shrouded in mystery. Was the anonymous commission of a Requiem a supernatural omen that it would be his own? Was he really poisoned? We'll probably never know.

Earlier in the year he had completed his last opera, *The Magic Flute*. This piece is played in the opera on small bells.

1791
Slave Dance

Wolfgang Amadeus Mozart
(1756–91)

1792
Minuet

The guillotine, a sinister device named after its inventor, Dr Guillotine, sent the first heads rolling in Paris. France became a republic, and the French National Anthem, *La Marseillaise*, was composed.

This minuet is from Haydn's 'Surprise' Symphony, so called because of an unexpected loud chord at the end of a quiet passage, designed to wake a snoozing audience.

Franz Joseph Haydn
(1732–1809)

1796
Menuetto

The British doctor Edmund Jenner used an eight-year-old boy as a human guinea-pig for the first vaccination. First he injected him with the contents of a milkmaid's cowpox pustule, and later with the deadly smallpox. The experiment was a success, and the boy's first injection made him immune to the second—luckily for both of them . . .

James Hook
(1746–1827)

Hook was an English composer and organist who composed over 2,000 songs.

4

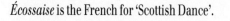

The composer Schumann was born this year. Initially he was just as interested in books, champagne, and girl-friends as in music, but he soon gave up a career in law for one as a pianist. However, he damaged his hand by using a mechanical device designed to strengthen it— a warning to all those inclined to over-practise.

Écossaise is the French for 'Scottish Dance'.

1810
Écossaise

Caspar Furstenau
(1772–1819)

The paddle-steamer *Savannah* was the first steamship to cross the Atlantic. Her arrival off the coast of Ireland caused consternation ashore: the smoke bellowing from her funnel made people think she was on fire and about to go down.

Beethoven arranged a number of folk-songs in variation form for flute and piano. This 'Russian Air' is called *Minka*.

1819
Air Russe

Ludwig van Beethoven
(1770–1827)

1828
Ländler

Franz Schubert
(1797–1827)

The Duke of Wellington—known for his famous boots—became the Prime Minister of Great Britain. Sir Charles Wheatsone perfected his design for the concertina, at one time so popular in high society that it had several professors of virtuoso ability.

The ländler was a German folk-dance which eventually developed into the waltz. It was a popular form with Schubert, who wrote many for the piano.

1848
Allegretto Cantabile

Giuseppe Concone
(1801–61)

This was the year of revolutions across Europe: from Berlin to Budapest, from Sicily to France, nationalist groups clamoured for independence. The Communist Manifesto was written in London by Karl Marx and Friedrich Engels.

Concone was a distinguished teacher, and composer of songs and singing exercises.

6

1860
Du, Du

Theobald Boehm
(1793–1881)

The Frenchman Lenoir invented the first practical internal combustion engine. Crinoline skirts and tiny waistlines were fashionable for women.

Boehm was the German flute virtuoso and composer who invented the fingering mechanism still in use on flutes today, while still finding time to superintend the Bavarian steel industry.

1868
Cradle Song

Johannes Brahms
(1833–97)

A skeleton of Cro-Magnon man was discovered in France, to great general excitement. A new game with shuttlecocks and racquets was developed at the Duke of Beaufort's Badminton House. In a year's time margarine will be invented!

Brahms was one of the greatest Romantic composers. This piece is an arrangement of one of his most famous songs, a lullaby so well known that most people assume it must be an old folk tune.

1881
Prithee, Pretty Maiden

Arthur Sullivan
(1842–1900)

In London, the Natural History Museum was opened.
Abroad, two world leaders were assassinated:
President Garfield of the USA and Tsar Alexander II of Russia.

This is an arrangement from the comic opera *Patience* which pokes fun at
the aesthetic movement personified by Oscar Wilde. Richard D'Oyly Carte,
owner of the Savoy Hotel, built the Savoy Theatre for the production of
works by Gilbert and Sullivan, later known as 'Savoy Operas'.

1892
My Son Eduardo

Enrique Granados
(1867–1916)

Keir Hardie became the first Labour MP in Great Britain. He
caused a stir in the House of Commons by wearing a cloth cap,
yellow tweed trousers, and a jacket, instead of the usual evening
dress. In a year's time, the first skyscraper will be built in Chicago.

Granados was a Spanish composer and virtuoso pianist.
He was killed on a liner torpedoed by a
German U-boat during World War I.

The Submerged Cathedral

Florence Nightingale, 'the lady with the lamp', died aged 90 and a national heroine. The world's first airline was launched—Zepplin airships flying from Berlin to Lake Constance on the borders of Germany and Switzerland.

This chorale-like piece is one of the composer's Piano Preludes. It suggests the legendary cathedral of Ys which rises out of the sea on certain clear mornings, the piano bottom C tolling like a great bell.

Claude Debussy
(1862–1918)

The Norwegian explorer Roald Amundsen and his team beat Captain Scott to the South Pole; Scott died in an attempt the following year.

Scott Joplin was known as the 'King of Ragtime' (an early type of jazz) and his best-known piano rags are played regularly today. The most famous is *The Entertainer* which was used as the title music to the film *The Sting* in the 1970s.

The Augustine Club Waltz

Scott Joplin
(1868–1917)

1912
Tovacov, Tovacov *

Leoš Janáček
(1854–1928)

The SS Titanic—supposedly unsinkable—struck an Atlantic iceberg on her maiden voyage; as the ship went down, its orchestra bravely played the hymn 'Abide with me'. Its underwater location remained undiscovered until the late 1980s.

Janáček was a prolific composer of operas and was interested in folk-music and speech rhythms. He carried a sketch-book with him so that he could write down interesting examples. This is a setting of a traditional Moravian folk-song.

1913
Two Pieces
1. What Little Princess Tulip Says
Erik Satie
(1866–1925)

Charlie Chaplin made his first film. The Suffragette Emily Davison threw herself fatally in front of the King's horse at the Derby, protesting for votes for women.

Satie, a French composer, was somewhat eccentric, as you can see from these pieces. He frequently gave his works unconventional titles and developed a uniquely individual style. Among his unusual interests was collecting umbrellas.

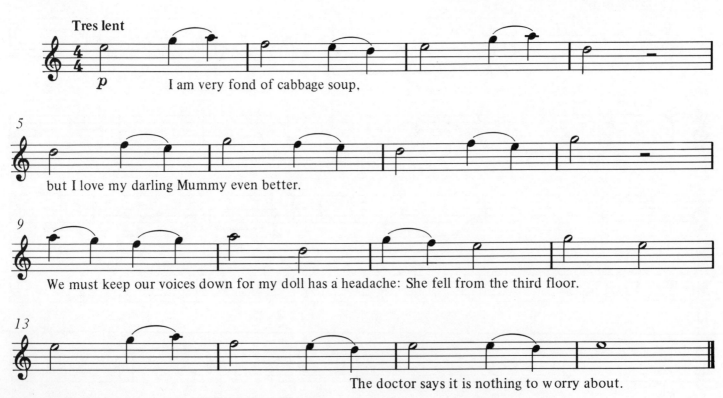

From "Five Moravian Dances" © EDITIO BÄRENREITER PRAHA, 1979

10

2. Pierrot's Berceuse

Lent

pp

At the end of the day, little Pierrot goes to bed.

He has been a very, very good boy.   His mother kisses

him.   He gets into bed,   pleased with himself, and says:

Retenir beaucoup

Will Grandpapa and Grandmama know that I've been very good?

Reprendre le mouvt.

Yes, replies Mama -

Who will tell them -

They will see it in the newspaper.

Little Pierrot goes to sleep, pleased as punch.

1990
Wistful Waltz

This is a short character-piece—so try and capture the mood suggested by the title. Follow the dynamics and tempo markings carefully (they'll help to convey the spirit of the music) and remember that this is a dance which needs a delicate, airy feel.

Paul Harris
(1957–   )

Reproduced and printed by
Halstan & Co. Ltd., Amersham, Bucks., England

MUSIC THROUGH TIME

PAUL HARRIS & SALLY ADAMS

FLUTE BOOK 1

CONTENTS

Christopher Columbus returned from his final voyage. Fifteenth-century geography was still a bit haphazard, and he died the following year in obscurity, believing the New World he had discovered—America—was off the coast of China!

Josquin was the greatest composer of the Renaissance, famous enough in his day to have his portrait painted by Leonardo da Vinci. 'El Grillo' is Spanish for 'the cricket', and this piece was originally a partsong about the insect's love of singing.

1505

El Grillo

Josquin Desprès
(c.1440–1521)

1612
Gavotte

Michael Praetorius
(1571–1612)

Bartholomew Legate and Edward Wightman were the last people to be burned at the stake for heresy in England. Also in England, a flag was flown at half-mast for the first time to signify a death—though not, sadly, that of the two unfortunate heretics.

This piece is from a set of dances Praetorius compiled for the Duke of Brunswick. He named the collection *Terpsichore*, after the Greek Muse of dancing.

Queen Anne died, having been the first monarch to rule over Great Britain after the Union of England and Scotland. She had had 17 children, all of whom died before they grew up, and was so fat when she was crowned that she had to be carried to her throne.

Though born in Germany, Handel lived for much of his life in England. With the composer Bononcini he founded the original Royal Academy of Music, a risky business venture to stage opera.

George Frideric Handel
(1685–1759)

1720
Bella Vittoria

Antonio Maria Bononcini

(1677–1726)

Wallpaper became fashionable in Britain. There was an early Stock Market crash when the 'South Sea Bubble'—a wild craze of financial speculation in the South Seas Trading Company—finally burst.

The composer of this piece was the brother of Handel's one-time business partner (see the previous piece): music was the Bononcini family business, with father and all three sons well-known composers.

Dr Samuel Johnson's *Dictionary of the English Language* appeared, the culmination of eight years' work. Unlike today's dictionaries, it contained only what he considered the 'best' words, defined with the aid of his prodigious memory and witty personal views.

Oswald was a Scottish composer, dancing master, string player, and publisher. This piece is taken from his collection of *Airs for the Four Seasons*.

Minuet

James Oswald
(c.1711–1769)

1791
Slave Dance

Wolfgang Amadeus Mozart
(1756–91)

Mozart died this year, in circumstances that are still shrouded in mystery. Was the anonymous commission of a Requiem a supernatural omen that it would be his own? Was he really poisoned? We'll probably never know.

Earlier in the year he had completed his last opera, *The Magic Flute*. This piece is played in the opera on small bells.

1792
Minuet

Franz Joseph Haydn
(1732–1809)

The guillotine, a sinister device named after its inventor, Dr Guillotine, sent the first heads rolling in Paris. France became a republic, and the French National Anthem, *La Marseillaise*, was composed.

This minuet is from Haydn's 'Surprise' Symphony, so called because of an unexpected loud chord at the end of a quiet passage, designed to wake a snoozing audience.

1796
Menuetto

James Hook
(1746–1827)

The British doctor Edmund Jenner used an eight-year-old boy as a human guinea-pig for the first vaccination. First he injected him with the contents of a milkmaid's cowpox pustule, and later with the deadly smallpox. The experiment was a success, and the boy's first injection made him immune to the second—luckily for both of them …

Hook was an English composer and organist who composed over 2,000 songs.

The composer Schumann was born this year. Initially he was just as interested in books, champagne, and girl-friends as in music, but he soon gave up a career in law for one as a pianist. However, he damaged his hand by using a mechanical device designed to strengthen it— a warning to all those inclined to over-practise.

Écossaise is the French for 'Scottish Dance'.

1810
Écossaise

Caspar Furstenau
(1772–1819)

1819
Air Russe

Ludwig van Beethoven
(1770–1827)

The paddle-steamer *Savannah* was the first steamship to cross the Atlantic. Her arrival off the coast of Ireland caused consternation ashore: the smoke bellowing from her funnel made people think she was on fire and about to go down.

Beethoven arranged a number of folk-songs in variation form for flute and piano. This 'Russian Air' is called *Minka*.

The Duke of Wellington—known for his famous boots—became
the Prime Minister of Great Britain. Sir Charles Wheatsone
perfected his design for the concertina, at one time so popular in
high society that it had several professors of virtuoso ability.

The ländler was a German folk-dance which eventually
developed into the waltz. It was a popular form with Schubert,
who wrote many for the piano.

Franz Schubert
(1797–1827)

15

1848
Allegretto Cantabile

Giuseppe Concone
(1801–61)

This was the year of revolutions across Europe: from Berlin to Budapest, from Sicily to France, nationalist groups clamoured for independence. The Communist Manifesto was written in London by Karl Marx and Friedrich Engels.

Concone was a distinguished teacher, and composer of songs and singing exercises.

1860 ^{2nd}
Du, Du

Theobald Boehm
(1793–1881)

The Frenchman Lenoir invented the first practical internal combustion engine. Crinoline skirts and tiny waistlines were fashionable for women.

Boehm was the German flute virtuoso and composer who invented the fingering mechanism still in use on flutes today, while still finding time to superintend the Bavarian steel industry.

1868
Cradle Song

Johannes Brahms
(1833–97)

A skeleton of Cro-Magnon man was discovered in France, to great general excitement. A new game with shuttlecocks and racquets was developed at the Duke of Beaufort's Badminton House. In a year's time margarine will be invented!

Brahms was one of the greatest Romantic composers. This piece is an arrangement of one of his most famous songs, a lullaby so well known that most people assume it must be an old folk tune.

In London, the Natural History Museum was opened.
Abroad, two world leaders were assassinated:
President Garfield of the USA and Tsar Alexander II of Russia.

This is an arrangement from the comic opera *Patience* which pokes fun at
the aesthetic movement personified by Oscar Wilde. Richard D'Oyly Carte,
owner of the Savoy Hotel, built the Savoy Theatre for the production of
works by Gilbert and Sullivan, later known as 'Savoy Operas'.

1881
Prithee, Pretty Maiden

Arthur Sullivan
(1842–1900)

1892
My Son Eduardo

Enrique Granados
(1867–1916)

Keir Hardie became the first Labour MP in Great Britain. He caused a stir in the House of Commons by wearing a cloth cap, yellow tweed trousers, and a jacket, instead of the usual evening dress. In a year's time, the first skyscraper will be built in Chicago.

Granados was a Spanish composer and virtuoso pianist. He was killed on a liner torpedoed by a German U-boat during World War I.

Florence Nightingale, 'the lady with the lamp', died aged 90 and a national heroine. The world's first airline was launched—Zepplin airships flying from Berlin to Lake Constance on the borders of Germany and Switzerland.

This chorale-like piece is one of the composer's Piano Preludes. It suggests the legendary cathedral of Ys which rises out of the sea on certain clear mornings, the piano bottom C tolling like a great bell.

Claude Debussy
(1862–1918)

1911
The Augustine Club Waltz

Scott Joplin
(1868–1917)

The Norwegian explorer Roald Amundsen and his team beat Captain Scott to the South Pole; Scott died in an attempt the following year.

Scott Joplin was known as the 'King of Ragtime' (an early type of jazz) and his best-known piano rags are played regularly today. The most famous is *The Entertainer* which was used as the title music to the film *The Sting* in the 1970s.

Allegretto

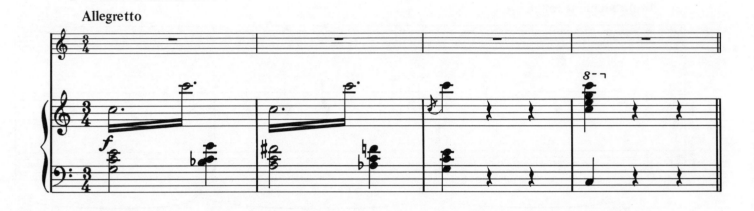

1912
Tovacov, Tovacov

Leoš Janáček
(1854–1928)

The SS Titanic—supposedly unsinkable—struck an Atlantic iceberg on her maiden voyage; as the ship went down, its orchestra bravely played the hymn 'Abide with me'. Its underwater location remained undiscovered until the late 1980s.

Janáček was a prolific composer of operas and was interested in folk-music and speech rhythms. He carried a sketch-book with him so that he could write down interesting examples. This is a setting of a traditional Moravian folk-song.

Charlie Chaplin made his first film. The Suffragette Emily Davison threw herself fatally in front of the King's horse at the Derby, protesting for votes for women.

Satie, a French composer, was somewhat eccentric, as you can see from these pieces. He frequently gave his works unconventional titles and developed a uniquely individual style. Among his unusual interests was collecting umbrellas.

1913
Two Pieces
1. What Little Princess Tulip Says
Erik Satie
(1866–1925)

2. Pierrot's Berceuse

Lent

pp

At the end of the day, little Pierrot goes to bed.

He has been a very, very good boy.   His mother kisses him.

He gets into bed,   pleased with himself, and says:

Retenir beaucoup

Will Grandpapa and Grandmama know that I've been very good?

1990
Wistful Waltz

This is a short character-piece—so try and capture the mood suggested by the title. Follow the dynamics and tempo markings carefully (they'll help to convey the spirit of the music) and remember that this is a dance which needs a delicate, airy feel.

Paul Harris
(1957-   )

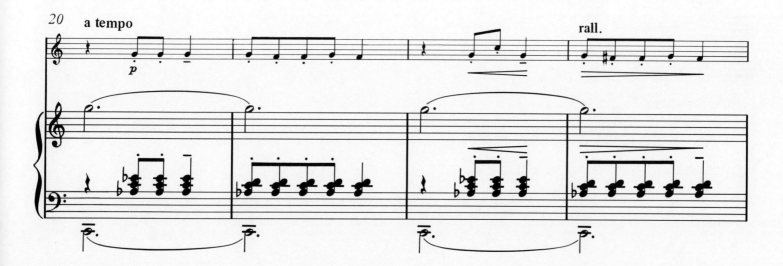

8va bassa